Wee McAsh to the Rescue

Written and Illustrated by Amanda Sunderland

For Sarah & Ash,

We did it! Well done ! We Three Musketeers x x

PS. We can have the dining room table back now.

With many, many Thanks to my family and friends for all their support and enthusiasm!

With love from 'Wee McAsh x

The sky is so blue, it's a bright sunny day.

Wee McAsh anchors his boat in the bay.

All of a sudden he hears a STRAMASH!

He looks up and sees a very big SPLASH!

He rows a bit nearer and now he can see

a seal pup stuck and she can't get free.

Fishing line tangled tight round her tail,

tugging and twisting the little pup wails.

The pup is in danger, don't delay!

Wee McAsh to the rescue right away!

Wee McAsh has a plan to set the pup free.

Can you guess what it is? Turn the page and you'll see.

Wee McAsh slowly moves the rock with an oar.

There's a gap and the water bursts through with a ROAR!

The rock breaks away, and the line falls free.

Well done Wee McAsh, you're as smart as can be!

Thanks Wee McAsh, you have worked hard today!

Our puppy is saved, HIP HIP HOORAY!

All back together, our seal family,

Mum, Dad and Pup wave goodbye happily.

Humming a tune as he rows merrily.

Soon Wee Mc Ash will be having his tea.

Full up and sleepy, all tucked in tight,

Wee McAsh is in bed now, so we'll say Good Night.

Sweet dreams

A WEE GLOSSARY

Glossary - a list of unusual words with their meanings explained in this book

Stramash - a Scottish word for a fuss

Stooshie - another Scottish word for a fuss
(not in this book but I just like saying it!)

and to finish off, Special Thanks to
Jayne and Shalla at Curly Tale Books,
Paula for getting me started
and in memory of Ernie The Isle's very own teller of tall tales.

FROM THE AUTHOR

Hello everyone and thank you for reading our wee seafaring tale based in the little village, The Isle of Whithorn in Dumfries and Galloway, Scotland. This is me and my wee dug, Ash, who inspired this story.

Ash is a smart cookie because he gives me all my ideas and you can see in the photograph above that I am listening very carefully to what he is telling me. This is taken on one of our favourite walks where we go to watch for the seals and dolphins, that we are lucky enough to see sometimes.

If you enjoyed reading this story, then look out for the next adventure which is coming soon! Bye for now.

Amanda Sunderland